MOTORMANIA

SPORTS CARS

ROB COLSON

WAYLAND
www.waylandbooks.co.uk

First published in Great Britain
in 2020 by Wayland
Copyright © Hodder and Stoughton, 2020
All rights reserved

Series editor: John Hort
Produced by Tall Tree Ltd
Designer: Jonathan Vipond

HB ISBN: 978 1 5263 1310 2
PB ISBN: 978 1 5263 1311 9

Wayland
An imprint of Hachette Children's Group
Part of Hodder and Stoughton
Carmelite House
50 Victoria Embankment
London EC4Y 0DZ

An Hachette UK Company
www.hachette.co.uk
www.hachettechildrens.co.uk

Printed and bound in China

Picture Credits
t-top, b-bottom, l-left, r-right, c-centre, fc-front cover,
bc-back cover
fc Aston Martin, bc Joseph Sohm / Shutterstock.com, 1 Honda,
2t Audi AG, 2c Honda, 2b BMW, 3t 3b Porsche AG, Jaguar Land
Rover Ltd, 4bl Daimler, 4-5 VanderWolf Images / Shutterstock.
com, 5tr Borgonovo Marco / Shutterstock.com, 5b Martin
Charles Hatch / Shutterstock.com, 6b Thesupermat / CC,
6-7 Ion Sebastian / Shutterstock.com, 7b Ion Sebastian /
Shutterstock.com, 8b Steve Lagreca / Shutterstock.com,
8-9, 9t Joseph Sohm / Shutterstock.com, 9b John Bauld / CC,
10c Hugh Llewelyn CC, 10-11, 10b, 11c Porsche AG, 11b Sudong
Kim / Shutterstock.com, 12-13t Gaschwald / Shutterstock.com,
12-13b Andy Glenn / Shutterstock.com, 13t Herranderssvensson
/ CC, 13b Karen Roe / CC, 14bl BigAlBaloo / Shutterstock.com,
14-15t, 14-15b, 15tr Mazda, 16b Vincent Doyle / Shutterstock.
com, 16-17t ermess / Shutterstock.com, 16-17b Toby Parsons /
Shutterstock.com, 17br Rahil Rupawala / CC, 18-19 Art
Konovalov / Shutterstock.com, 18bl, 19tr, 19br Audi AG, 20t ibrar.
kunri / Shutterstock.com, 20cr Matti Blume / CC, 20bl RikoBest /
Shutterstock.com, 21tr, 21r, 32b Jaguar Land Rover Ltd, 22bl,
22-23t, 22-23b, 23c, 23r BMW, 24-25, 24b, 25cl, 25t, 25br Honda,
26-27, 27t, 27c, 27b Aston Martin, 28-29, 29t, 29b Ethos.lee /
Shutterstock.com

MIX
Paper from
responsible sources
FSC® C104740
www.fsc.org

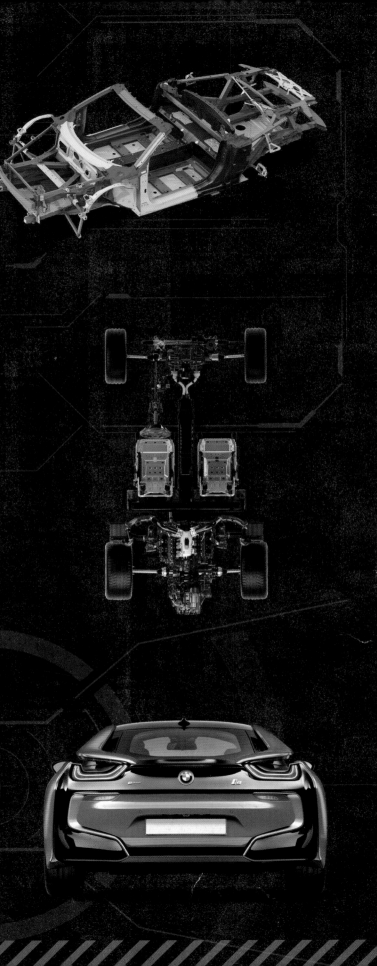

CONTENTS

WHAT IS A SPORTS CAR?

Sports cars are stylish vehicles made to look good and move quickly. They are usually small cars with just two seats. With sharp handling and powerful engines, they give the driver the feel of a racing car.

THE FIRST SPORTS CAR

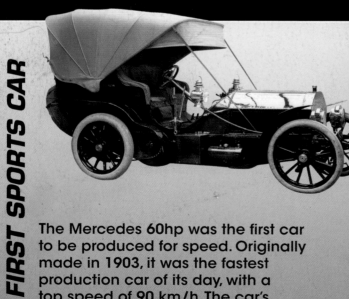

The Mercedes 60hp was the first car to be produced for speed. Originally made in 1903, it was the fastest production car of its day, with a top speed of 90 km/h. The car's 60 **horsepower (hp)** was generated by a huge 9.2 litre, four-**cylinder** engine.

IMPROVING PERFORMANCE

Manufacturers are constantly seeking to improve their cars' performance. In the 1980s, **turbochargers** were added to the engines of many sports cars. These force extra air into the cylinders to increase their power. In recent years, new high-tech materials, such as **carbon-fibre reinforced plastic**, have been developed to make the car bodies and **chassis** lighter and to increase speed.

The Alfa Romeo 4C is a modern sports car with a light carbon-fibre and aluminium body and a turbocharged engine.

ROAD AND TRACK
Many sports cars are designed both for the road and for racing on the track. They are often stripped of any extras to save weight. They are also given a stiff **suspension**, to improve **handling**, and have parts such as rear wings added to improve **aerodynamics**.

STYLE ICONS

Some sports cars have become famous because of their unique, stylish designs. The Jaguar E-Type, made from 1961 to 1975, is widely considered to be one of the best cars ever, and is a highly desired collector's item.

A Jaguar E-Type Convertible

ALFA ROMEO
6C 2500

Italian manufacturer Alfa Romeo created some of the best sports cars of the 1930s and 1940s. The 6C 2500 was a range of six-cylinder cars. They were famed for their reliability, and many are still running.

MANY MAKERS

Alfa Romeo designed the basic shape and engine of the 6C 2500, but it was hand-built by a number of small companies across Italy. For this reason, many slightly different versions of the car exist. All of them feature Alfa Romeo's distinctive triangular front grille.

TECH POINT

In 1948, Alfa Romeo produced a racing version of the 6C 2500 called the Competizione Berlinetta. They cut down the frame of the car to save weight and fitted it with a more powerful engine to produce a top speed of 200 km/h. Three models were built, of which just one survives today. It sold in 2018 for £2.7 million.

The car was shortened by 20 mm to improve its cornering ability.

6C 2500

Wide mudguards

Running boards were fitted to some models to help passengers climb in and out.

YEARS OF PRODUCTION:
(1938–1952)

ENGINE:
2.5 litre, 6 cylinders

POWER:
90 hp

TOP SPEED:
155 km/h

0–100 KM/H:
16 seconds

GOLDEN ARROW

Produced from 1946, the Freccia d'Oro (Italian for 'Golden Arrow') was the most successful version of the 6C 2500, with more than 600 models made. Stylish and very expensive, it was built more for luxury than for speed. The Freccia d'Oro was a status symbol in the 1940s, with owners that included kings and movie stars.

CHEVROLET
CORVETTE C1

In 1953, to compete with the stylish cars arriving in the USA from Europe, General Motors (GM) created the Chevrolet Corvette, a curvy two-seater convertible. The first generation of the Corvette, the C1, was produced until 1962.

In 1958, the car was given twin headlights and extra chrome trim, following the fashion of the day.

TECH POINT

The body of the first Corvette C1 was made from fibreglass. First developed as a building material in 1936, fibreglass is a mix of glass and plastic that is strong but lightweight. However, customers reported faults in the bodywork and disliked its rough finish.

A 1955 Corvette C1

MOUNTAIN RACE

The 1953 Corvette looked the part, but it was less powerful than its European equivalents and GM struggled to sell it. This all changed in 1955 when Chevrolet's Director of High Performance, Zora Arkus-Duntov, replaced the **automatic** 6-cylinder engine with a **manual** 8-cylinder engine. This added 45 hp. Arkus-Duntov, who was also a racing driver, showcased the new model's abilities by setting a new record time for a **stock car** in the annual 'Race to the Clouds' hill climb at Pikes Peak, Colorado.

This open-top convertible sports car could be fitted with a soft or hard removable roof.

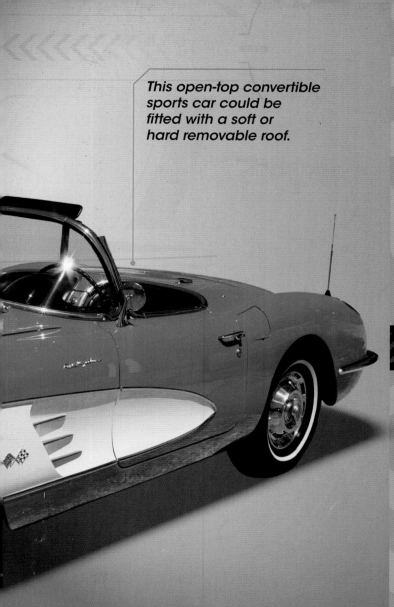

CORVETTE C1

YEARS OF PRODUCTION:
1953–1962 (first generation)

ENGINE:
2.65 litre, 8 cylinders (from 1955)

POWER:
195 hp

TOP SPEED:
195 km/h

0–100 KM/H:
9 seconds

MODERN CORVETTE
The seventh generation of the Corvette is is called the C7 ZR1 (right). It went on sale in 2019. With a top speed of more than 340 km/h, this is a limited-edition, high-performance **supercar**. It is fitted with aerodynamic features that have been perfected in tests in a wind tunnel.

The rear wing adds downforce.

The air intakes keep the tyres cool.

PORSCHE
911

With more than 1 million cars produced since 1963, the 911 is Porsche's most popular car and one of the most successful sports cars ever. The model has been continually updated, while maintaining the same distinctive shape.

The powerful 911 Carrera RS was made in 1973 for racing.

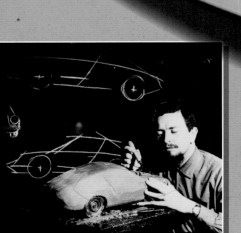

CREATING THE SHAPE
The 911 was developed from sketches made in 1959 by Ferdinand 'Butzi' Porsche (1935–2012, left), Butzi was the grandson of Ferdinand Porsche, the founder of the company and designer of the VW Beetle.

EIGHTH-GENERATION 911

Each new generation of 911 builds on the last. The eighth-generation 911 (left), produced in 2019, features a powerful 3-litre turbocharged engine that delivers 444 hp and a top speed of 307 km/h. It has been engineered to give better weight distribution, improving handling at high speeds.

TECH POINT

The engine of the 911 sits above the rear axle. The extra weight at the rear gives the car excellent grip when it accelerates. However, it also makes it harder to handle. Up to 1998, the engine was cooled by air, but it was prone to overheating when standing in traffic, as air could not pass through the engine. This system was replaced in 1998 by a water-cooling system, in which water is pumped through passages in the engine block.

The engine is behind the rear wheels.

911

YEARS OF PRODUCTION:
1963–1998 (air-cooled engine)

ENGINE:
2.0–3.3 litre, 4–6 cylinders

POWER:
130 hp (1963)

TOP SPEED:
210 km/h

0–100 KM/H:
8.5 seconds

LOTUS ESPRIT

This wedge-shaped sports car from UK manufacturer Lotus had the sharp angles that were typical of 1970s design. Small, light and extremely nimble, the Esprit was famous for its great handling.

ESPRIT

PRODUCTION:
1976–2004 (Series 1: 1976–1978)

ENGINE:
2 litre, 4 cylinders (Series 1)

POWER:
162 hp

TOP SPEED:
214 km/h

0–100 KM/H:
8 seconds

Pop-up headlights

The Maserati Boomerang concept car

'FOLDED PAPER'

The Esprit was designed by Italian Giorgetto Giugiaro (born 1938). He based its look on the Boomerang, a **concept car** he had developed for Maserati in 1971. Giugiaro's angular style became known as the 'folded paper'. He would later create similar designs for the BMW M1 and the DMC DeLorean.

The wedge-shaped design was very aerodynamic.

TECH POINT

To produce top performance, Lotus concentrated on keeping their cars as light as possible. The Esprit's lightweight fibreglass body was mounted on a tubular steel chassis. The engine was placed behind the driver, as in a racing car, to give great balance. With only four cylinders, the engine was small and light. The car weighed just 900 kg, and it quickly gained a reputation for excellent handling, even though it lacked the power of a larger car.

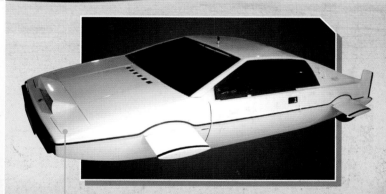

BOND SUBMARINE
The Esprit featured in the 1977 Bond movie The Spy Who Loved Me *with a special 'submarine mode'. To film the Esprit transforming itself into a sub, seven different models were made. The final car seen in the movie was a fully operational submarine.*

MAZDA
RX-7

This small Japanese sports car packed a punch in performance. The first generation sold nearly half a million models, but it is a rare sight on the roads today as its compact engine lacked durability.

SMALL BUT POWERFUL

The RX-7 was designed primarily for the home market in Japan, where large cars are taxed heavily. The tiny Wankel engine complied with Japanese tax rules while producing good power. It sat just behind the front axle, giving the car great balance, and the RX-7 became popular for its handling.

TECH POINT

Most car engines contain cylinders, inside which fuel burns to create pressure that pumps pistons up and down. In a Wankel engine, fuel is burnt to create a circular motion. Inside an oval-shaped chamber, a three-sided rotor turns around a central shaft. On one side of the chamber, spark plugs ignite the fuel. On the other side, fuel enters through the intake, and fumes leave through the exhaust.

Intake

Spark plugs

Rotation

Central shaft

Exhaust

FATHER AND SON

The chief designer of the first generation RX-7 was Matasaburo Maeda, who was inspired by the compact wedge-shaped design of the Lotus Esprit (see pages 12–13). Maeda's son, Ikuo, took over as head of design at Mazda in 2000, and was responsible for producing the RX-8, the car that replaced the RX-7 in 2003.

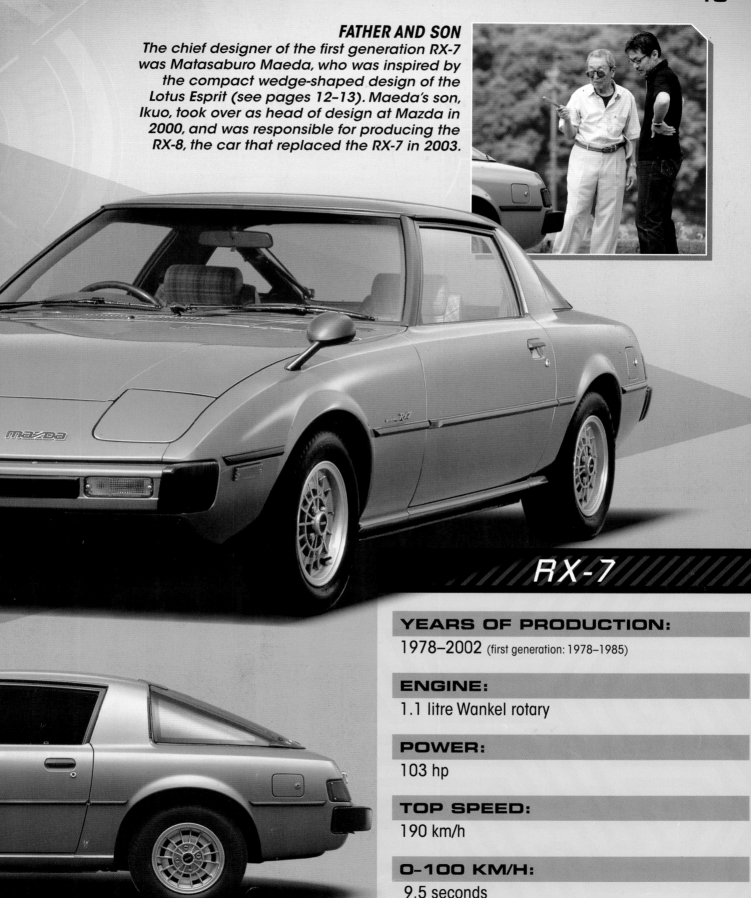

RX-7

YEARS OF PRODUCTION:

1978–2002 (first generation: 1978–1985)

ENGINE:

1.1 litre Wankel rotary

POWER:

103 hp

TOP SPEED:

190 km/h

0–100 KM/H:

9.5 seconds

FERRARI
F40

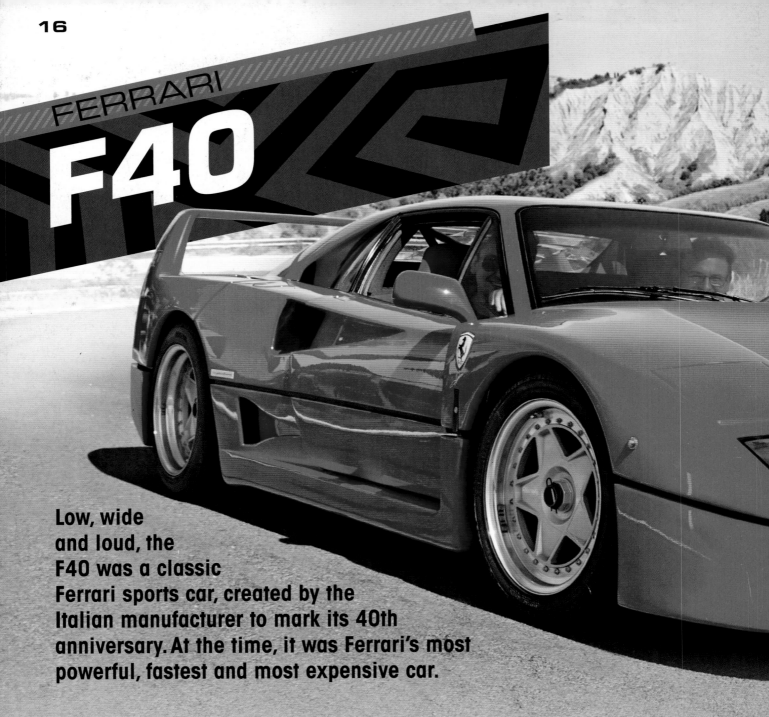

Low, wide
and loud, the
F40 was a classic
Ferrari sports car, created by the
Italian manufacturer to mark its 40th
anniversary. At the time, it was Ferrari's most
powerful, fastest and most expensive car.

BUILT FOR SPEED

To keep weight to a minimum, the F40
came with very few frills. There was no
sound system, although you would have
struggled to hear the radio over the
roaring engine. There were no carpets
or glove box, and it had only minimal
air conditioning.

TECH POINT

To maximise power, the engine was fitted with turbochargers, which pushed extra air into the cylinders. This generated a lot of heat. To keep the engine cool, the body was shaped to allow plenty of air to pass around the engine. Wide vents either side of the car directed air over the engine, which sat behind the driver.

F40

YEARS OF PRODUCTION:
1987–1992

ENGINE:
2.9 litre, 8 cylinders

POWER:
471 hp

TOP SPEED:
321 km/h

0–100 KM/H:
4.1 seconds

RACING MODEL

Ferrari produced 19 extra-powerful models of the F40 for track racing. With an upgraded engine producing 691 hp, the racing car had a top speed of 367 km/h. Today, these models are highly prized collectors' items. One was sold in 2019 for more than £4 million.

Twin exhaust pipes sit either side of a pipe from the turbochargers.

AUDI
R8

The Audi R8 is a mid-engine sports car. The original Type 42 model was made with the same chassis as the more expensive Lamborghini Gallardo. In 2015, Audi replaced it with the more powerful Type 4S.

Laser spot lights in each headlight provide long-distance visibility.

SMART LIGHTS

The R8 was the first production car to be fitted with all-**LED** headlights. The high-beam unit is made of 25 individual sections, which can be brightened or dimmed according to the situation. When sensors spot another car approaching, the unit automatically dims the lights shining at that car to avoid dazzling the oncoming driver.

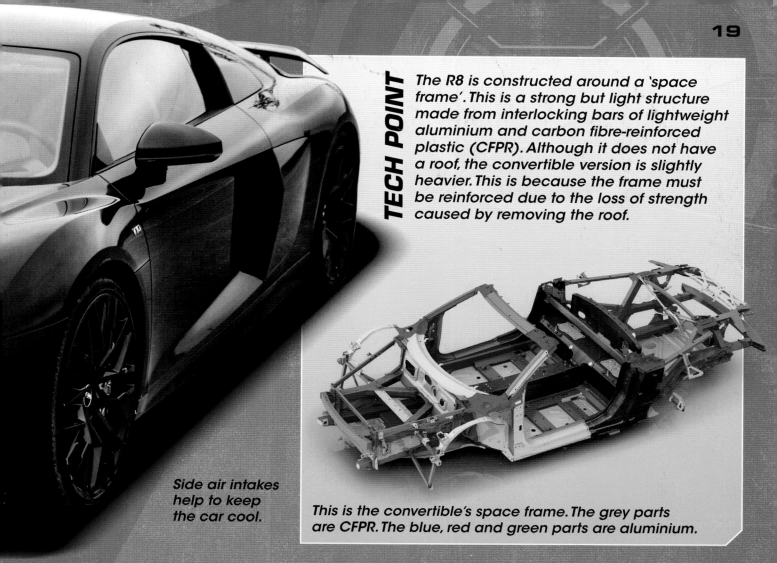

TECH POINT

The R8 is constructed around a 'space frame'. This is a strong but light structure made from interlocking bars of lightweight aluminium and carbon fibre-reinforced plastic (CFPR). Although it does not have a roof, the convertible version is slightly heavier. This is because the frame must be reinforced due to the loss of strength caused by removing the roof.

Side air intakes help to keep the car cool.

This is the convertible's space frame. The grey parts are CFPR. The blue, red and green parts are aluminium.

R8

YEARS OF PRODUCTION:
2006–2015 (Type 42); 2015– (Type 4S)

ENGINE:
4.2 litre, 8 cylinders (Type 42)

POWER:
414 hp

TOP SPEED:
301 km/h

0–100 KM/H:
4.6 seconds

MARVEL MOTOR
The Audi R8 has appeared in many different Marvel movies, most notably the Iron Man trilogy. In Iron Man III, the Iron Man, played by actor Robert Downey Jnr (above), drives a **prototype** all-electric model called the R8 e-tron.

JAGUAR
F-TYPE

Intended as the successor to the E-Type (see page 5), the F-Type is Jaguar's fastest sports car. Built around an all-aluminium body and suspension system, the car includes some of the latest high-tech features.

IAN CALLUM
Scot Ian Callum (born 1954) submitted a design to Jaguar in 1968 aged just 14, in the hope it would land him a job. He joined the company 30 years later as Director of Design. Before joining Jaguar, Callum designed the DB7 and Vanquish for Aston Martin.

PROJECT 7

In 2014, Jaguar produced a limited edition of a convertible F-Type called Project 7 (right). With a 5-litre turbocharged engine, it was Jaguar's fastest-ever production car. The car was kitted out in specially developed aerodynamic parts and fitted with race-inspired bucket seats.

F-TYPE

YEARS OF PRODUCTION:
2013–

ENGINE:
2 litre, 4 cylinders (300PS version)

POWER:
296 hp

TOP SPEED:
250 km/h (electronically limited)

0–100 KM/H:
5.7 seconds

TECH POINT

The F-Type is made for maximum style and safety. In the event of a crash, its aluminium body has parts that are designed to crumple to reduce the force on the passengers. If the car hits a pedestrian, sensors in the bumper trigger two small airbags, which lift the bonnet by a few centimetres to soften the blow.

BMW i8

The BMW i8 is the world's best-selling hybrid sports car. A hybrid vehicle is powered by both a petrol engine and an electric motor. In addition to its motor, the i8 is packed with the latest technology, including laser headlights.

REDUCING CARBON DIOXIDE

Hybrid cars like the i8 are more environmentally friendly. In a car with just a petrol engine, all its energy comes from burning fuel, which releases the **greenhouse gas** carbon dioxide into the atmosphere. This contributes to climate change. Powerful sports cars with just a petrol engine give off more than 300 grams of carbon dioxide every kilometre (g/km). On average, the BMW i8 gives off just 49 g/km.

TECH POINT

The rear wheels of the i8 are powered by the engine, while the electric motor turns the front wheels, taking its energy from a battery. The battery can be charged from a power socket, and it is also charged while the car is on the move by recovering energy from the brakes. The engine, motor and battery are arranged across the car to give it perfect balance.

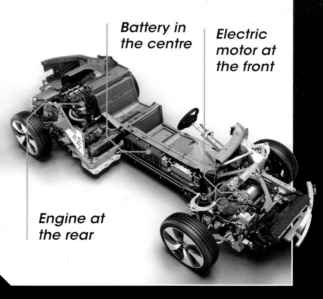

Battery in the centre

Electric motor at the front

Engine at the rear

The 'butterfly' doors open upwards, allowing access to the car in tight spaces.

YEARS OF PRODUCTION:
2014–

ENGINE:
1.5 litre, 3 cylinders, plus an electric motor

POWER:
engine 228 hp; motor 129 hp

TOP SPEED:
limited to 250 km/h

0–100 KM/H:
4.4 seconds

PRINTED PARTS
BMW make some of the smaller components of the i8, such as the roof attachments, on a 3D printer. 3D printing allows complex shapes to be made to a very high level of precision. The parts are built up, layer by layer, out of plastic or metal, by computer-controlled robotic arms.

HONDA NSX

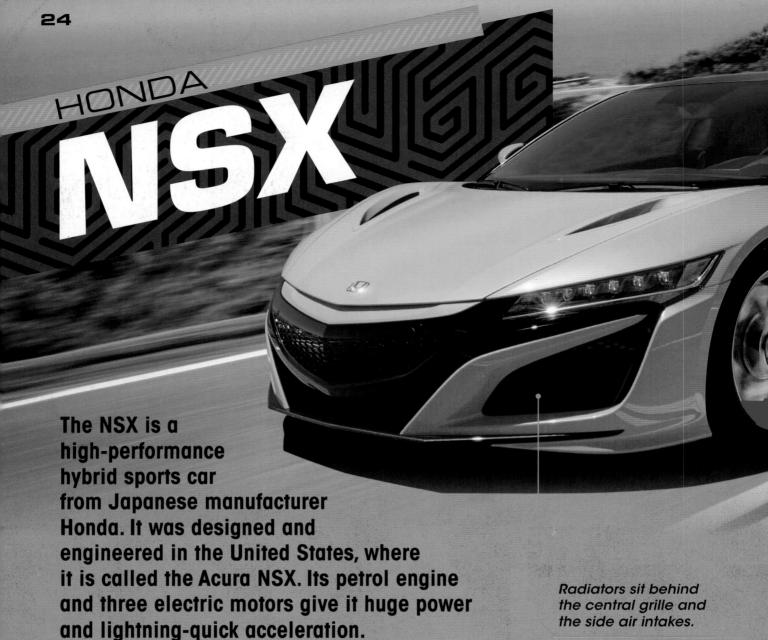

The NSX is a high-performance hybrid sports car from Japanese manufacturer Honda. It was designed and engineered in the United States, where it is called the Acura NSX. Its petrol engine and three electric motors give it huge power and lightning-quick acceleration.

Radiators sit behind the central grille and the side air intakes.

TED KLAUS

American engineer Ted Klaus (born 1963) led the team that developed the NSX. Always interested in speed, Klaus ensured that the design maximised the car's performance. The NSX combines sleek good looks and high performance with good fuel economy. Klaus describes it as an 'everyday supercar'.

NSX

YEARS OF PRODUCTION:
2016–

ENGINE:
3.5 litre, 6 cylinders; 3 electric motors

POWER:
573 hp

TOP SPEED:
307 km/h

0–100 KM/H:
2.9 seconds

An NSX factory workstation

HAND-MADE
The NSX is manufactured in a factory in Ohio, USA. The factory is an open space with workstations at which teams of highly skilled workers assemble the parts. They use an 'inside-out' process in which the interior is assembled first. The electrical systems are installed before the body is built around it. Robots take over at the end to ensure a perfect paint job.

Twin motor unit at the front

POWER BOOST
Most of the power of the NSX comes from its petrol engine. At moments when the car needs extra power, a central electric motor can assist the engine to drive the rear wheels. Each front wheel is driven independently by its own electric motor.

Battery

Engine

ASTON MARTIN
DBS SUPERLEGGERA

The large honeycomb grille dominates the front of the car. It allows plenty of air into the engine.

This powerful grand tourer is UK manufacturer Aston Martin's fastest and slickest car. The DBS Superleggera is a larger, faster version of a previous Aston Martin car, the DB11.

GRAND TOURER

A grand tourer (GT) is a large two-seater that combines high performance with a smooth driving experience. The engine of a GT is usually at the front to leave extra room for the cabin and a boot at the back. Aston Martin became famous in the 1950s for their luxurious, stylish and expensive GTs.

TECH POINT

To give the car good grip, Aston Martin developed a system called the Aeroblade. Openings behind the rear windows trap air flowing on the side of the car. Ducts direct the air to the rear, where it leaves through a thin slit. The exiting air rushes out upwards, creating a force that presses down on the rear wheels.

DRIVING MODES

The DBS Superleggera can be driven in three different modes. The normal mode provides maximum comfort, with soft suspension for a smooth ride. The two sport modes stiffen up the suspension and make the steering more responsive. This gives a much bumpier ride, but improves the car's handling.

DBS SUPERLEGGERA

The luxurious seats are upholstered in soft leather.

YEARS OF PRODUCTION:
2018–

ENGINE:
5.2 litre, 12 cylinders

POWER:
715 hp

TOP SPEED:
340 km/h

0–100 KM/H:
3.4 seconds

QIANTU
K50

The K50 is an all-electric sports car from China. It is powered by two electric motors, one over the front axle and the other over the rear axle. The car has the look of a supercar, but sells for a fraction of the price.

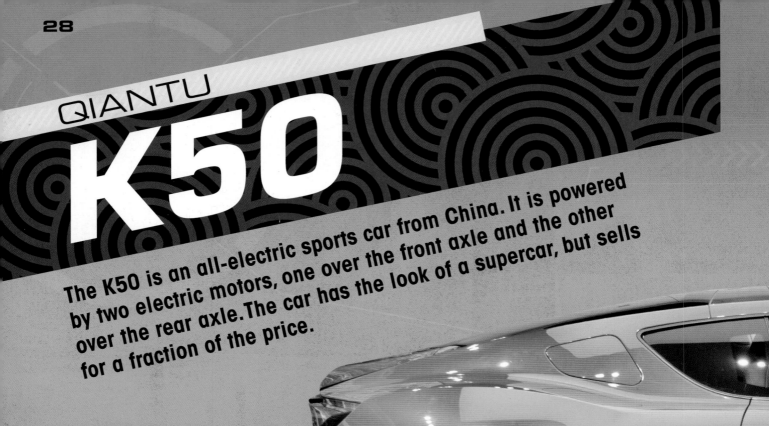

K50

YEARS OF PRODUCTION:
2018–

MOTORS:
Two motors, 580 Nm (**Newton metres**)

POWER:
376 hp from two electric motors

TOP SPEED:
200 km/h

0–100 KM/H:
4.6 seconds

RANGE ON ONE CHARGE:
365 km

NEW COMPANY

Qiantu (meaning 'future' in Chinese) was founded in 2015 with a mission to develop high-performance electric cars. To produce the K50, the company has built a new factory in Suzhou, China, which will make 50,000 cars a year. Initially, the car was only available in China, but, in 2020, Qiantu expanded production to the United States with a factory in California.

The air conditioning is powered by a solar panel on the roof.

Inside, the driver can change the car's settings via a large touchscreen.

The body is made from lightweight carbon fibre, mounted over an aluminium frame.

Alloy wheels save weight.

TECH POINT

One of the biggest problems facing manufacturers of electric cars is the vehicle's range. This is the distance it can travel before it has to stop to recharge the batteries. Larger batteries last longer, but they also add weight. Qiantu are developing a lithium battery that is 30 per cent lighter than current batteries. If their tests are successful, the new batteries will boost the K50's range by a further 100 km.

GLOSSARY

Aerodynamics
The way in which an object moves through air. Engineers study aerodynamics to produce cars that allow air to move around them smoothly.

Alloy
A material made from a mix of different metals.

Automatic
A car with a gearbox that changes gear automatically.

Carbon-fibre reinforced plastic (CFRP)
A strong but lightweight material made from plastic with thin strands of carbon woven into it.

Chassis
The strong frame of a car to which the engine, wheels and body are attached.

Concept car
A vehicle made to show off a new design or new technology. Concept cars are often made to be displayed at motor shows.

Cylinders
The parts of an engine inside which fuel burns to pump pistons up and down and generate power.

Downforce
A force produced by air resistance that pushes down on a moving vehicle. Downforce keeps a car safely on the road.

Greenhouse gas
A gas that contributes to global warming if it is released into the atmosphere.

Handling
The ease with which a driver can control a car.

Horsepower (hp)
A unit of measurement for power, or the rate at which work is done.

LED
Short for Light-Emitting Diode. A device that gives off light when electricity is passed through it.

Manual
A car with a gearbox that is controlled by the driver.

Newton metre
A unit of measurement for turning force.

Prototype
A model of a new design that is made to test out the design.

Running boards
Platforms fitted to the sides of old cars to help people to climb in.

Stock car
An ordinary road car that has been strengthened for racing.

Supercar
A high-performance sports car that is made in small numbers and sells for a high price.

Suspension
A system of springs and shock absorbers that attach the wheels to a car's chassis.

Turbocharger
A device, powered by the exhaust, that increases the pressure of the air that is fed into an engine's cylinders. This helps the fuel to burn, increasing the power of the engine.

SPORTS CARS THAT MADE HISTORY

YEAR	MODEL	MANUFACTURER	COUNTRY	TOP SPEED	SPORTS CAR FIRST
1903	60hp	Mercedes	Germany	90 km/h	First production car made for speed
1923	Type-U3	Chennard-Walcker	France	150 km/h	Won the first Le Mans 24 Hour endurance race
1949	XK120	Jaguar	UK	200 km/h	First production car to break the 200 km/h barrier
1951	G2	Glasspar	USA	170 km/h (approx.)	First sports car with an all-fibreglass body
1953	550 Spyder	Porsche	Germany	220 km/h	First rear-engine sports car
1962	Jetfire	Oldsmobile	USA	176 km/h	First sports car to be fitted with a turbocharger
1964	NSU Spider	NSU	Germany	153 km/h	First production car with a Wankel rotary engine
1983	Ruf BTR	Porsche	Germany	305 km/h	First production car to break the 300 km/h barrier
1991	EB110	Bugatti	France	336 km/h	First sports car with a carbon-fibre monocoque chassis
2005	Veyron EB16.4	Bugatti	France	408 km/h	First production car to break the 400 km/h barrier
2008	Roadster	Tesla	USA	201 km/h	First all-electric sports car
2010	Cr-Z	Honda	Japan	201 km/h	First hybrid sports car

INDEX